Original title:
Frosted Gingerbread Nights

Copyright © 2024 Creative Arts Management OÜ
All rights reserved.

Author: Tobias Sterling
ISBN HARDBACK: 978-9916-90-856-3
ISBN PAPERBACK: 978-9916-90-857-0

The Glow of Sugared Twilight

Under the stars, the cookies dance,
Whisked in laughter, in a sugary trance.
Frosting's a hat, icing's a coat,
The doughnuts spin in their jolly float.

Marzipan moons wobble with glee,
While licorice lights buzz like a bee.
Sugar plum fairies, in their pastry wink,
Toast to the night with a fizzy drink.

Snowflakes in the Bakery

In the chaos of flour, a snowflake sneezed,
Pastry chefs laughed, slightly displeased.
Rolling pins twirled, like dancers in rows,
Crafting sweet chaos, in drizzles and glows.

Cinnamon sprinkles like confetti at play,
Ginger snaps giggle, 'We'll seize the day!'
Cookie cutters clink, a jolly parade,
While cupcakes are building their sugary brigade.

A Hearth of Sweetened Wishes

The oven hums a tune, soft and mild,
As gumdrops gather, all rosy and wild.
S'mores on the mantle, marshmallows cheer,
Wishing for laughter, bringing good cheer.

As the timers chime a whimsically tune,
Brownies jump up, like they're over the moon.
A gingerbread man takes a playful fall,
Spreading sweet moments, inviting us all.

Glimmers of Gingerbread Magic

Hot cocoa bubbles with a sugary grin,
While marshmallows tumble, inviting to sink.
A merry old elf on a cookie spree,
Is painting the night with icing, you'll see.

Chocolate chips scatter like stars on the floor,
Each silly mischief, we'll always adore.
Strawberries giggle while jellies collide,
These sugary dreams, we'll take in our stride.

Sweet Shadows in the Snow

In the quiet of the night, so bright,
Snowflakes dance in the pale moonlight.
Giggling children in hats so tight,
Building snowmen, what a silly sight.

Hot cocoa spills, a drippy fate,
Marshmallows dive, oh, what a plate!
Snowball fights lead to bellyache,
But laughter echoes, it's worth the break.

Sleds go zooming, like wild geese,
Whoops and yelps, won't find our peace.
Slipping and sliding, 'gainst all release,
Laughter ignites, a joyful fleece.

So toast to the snow, cheers to the cheer,
With playful bumbles, we hold so dear.
Each frosty moment brings winter near,
As sweet shadows frolic, season's premier.

Spiced Memories of Yule

Ginger whirls in warm, spiced air,
Laughter echoes, without a care.
Cookies crumble, a sugary flare,
Whiskers twitch on every chair.

Elves in pajamas, mismatched socks,
Unruly chaos, like ticking clocks.
Gifts unwrapped, and much to mock,
Silly dances 'round the blocks.

Nutmeg sprinkles on pancakes tall,
Cats chase ribbons, pawing the hall.
Oops! There goes the last meatball,
Oopsie daisies, we had a ball!

This merry Yuletide, let's raise a cheer,
With quirky spiced tales we hold so dear.
In cozy corners, friends draw near,
Sharing joy as the bright lights appear.

A Night of Caramelized Stars

Under a sky so deep and wide,
Stars like candies, all twinkling tied.
Whispers of sweet with moon as guide,
Dreams dip low on a merry ride.

Caramel drips on the crooked tree,
Casually bubbling with wild glee.
Swinging from branches, a sweet decree,
Playing tag with the bumblebee.

Cookies on paper plates piled high,
Mouths agape as laughter flies.
Falling back in the snow, oh my!
With sticky fingers, we reach for the sky.

So let's toast to nights that delight,
With sprinkles of joy, oh what a sight!
Every sticky moment feels just right,
In this candy-coated frosty night.

Candied Footprints in the Frost

Footprints march in the blanket white,
Tiny wonders in morning light.
Squeals erupt at the softest sight,
Scavenger hunts bring sheer delight.

Gumdrops hidden, a treasure hunt,
Searching giggles, the cheeky stunt.
Sweet surprise where there's no front,
Silly faces, the load is blunt.

Chasing shadows with sticky hands,
Creating castles and frosty bands.
Candy canes and gumdrops in strands,
With sugary proof across the lands.

So let's dance in this sugary frost,
Every giggle shared feels like a boast.
In laughter's embrace, we're never lost,
With candied footprints, we're happy hosts.

Dancing Shadows of Nutmeg Dreams

In the kitchen, spices twirl,
Flour flies as whiskers whirl.
Ginger snaps and cookies grin,
While the dance begins again.

Silly elves with sugar hats,
Spilling milk and laughing cats.
Merry jokes in a sweet trance,
Baking's always a silly dance.

Frosty windows, giggles loud,
A cookie army—feeling proud.
Nutmeg whispers, chocolate winks,
Laughter echoes as the dough sinks.

So gather 'round, let's celebrate,
With dough and laughter on our plate.
Bake your dreams, let go of strife,
In our silly, sugary life.

Hearthside Memories Wrapped in Dough

The oven hums a cozy tune,
Baking rhythms like a boon.
Laughter bakes into the air,
Hearthside fun and cozy flair.

Rolling pins go whack and smack,
Sugar sprinkles make a snack.
Grandma's tales, a sweet reprise,
While the dough begins to rise.

Cinnamon swirls and giggles blend,
Every batch, a joyful trend.
Sticky fingers, chocolate trails,
These are where the fun prevails.

With every bite, a memory's spun,
A heartwarming laugh, a family run.
Wrapping loves in doughy charms,
Together safe in warmest arms.

Laughter and Sprinkles Under Stars

Under stars, the sprinkles rain,
Cookies dance without a pain.
Chocolate rivers, marshmallow dreams,
Giggles echo in silent streams.

Silly hats and gingerbread men,
Make a joke and laugh again.
Frosty air, yet warmth inside,
With every bite, the world's a ride.

Golden crusts and sticky hands,
Baking joys form happy bands.
With each snicker and playful cheer,
This is the magic we hold dear.

Sprinkle parties, oh what fun,
Underneath the moon's sweet run.
Laughter flows, the dough will rise,
In our baked, sugary skies.

An Ode to Honey and Hearths

Oh honey, sweet on every plate,
Hearthside chaos, never late.
Sticky jars and giggling spry,
As cookies puff and children sigh.

Rolling dough with fumbles bold,
A sprinkle fight, the tales retold.
Doughy hats upon our heads,
Silly laughter fills our beds.

Caramel drizzle, oh so fun,
Slipping smiles, we must run.
Honey drips and mock debate,
In our hearts we celebrate.

From the oven, joy unveiled,
Honey hugs that never failed.
Let us toast a laughter's toast,
In this warmth, we love the most.

Festive Echoes Beneath the Pines

Under twinkling lights we dance,
With cookies close, we take a chance.
A sneaky bite, oh what delight,
The sugar rush will last all night.

The tree is tall, the gifts are wide,
But watch your step, my friends, oh my!
A tumble here, a giggle there,
Our holiday spirit fills the air.

With sprinkles flying everywhere,
A little frosting in our hair.
We wear our treats, a sight to see,
Who needs a hat when sweet's for free?

Laughter echoes through the hall,
As cookie people start to sprawl.
They tell us jokes, absurd and grand,
The funniest feast in all the land!

The Spice of Fairy Tales

In a cottage made of candy bliss,
A lively chef is hard to miss.
With flour clouds and doughy fights,
He dreams of treats on starry nights.

His apron's stained with icing flair,
He whistles tunes, without a care.
But when the batter starts to flop,
He laughs it off and does a hop.

With rolling pins as swords in hand,
The cookies battle—what a band!
They march right out, brave little bites,
In wild adventures, full of sights.

But when the oven dings, oh dear,
The sweet smell tells us fun is near.
We gather round, our laughter flies,
As every nibble brings surprise!

Sugarplum Reveries at Dusk

As the sun dips low, in pink and gold,
A tale of cookies starts to unfold.
With pixie dust and candy canes,
The merriment dances in our veins.

A sugar rush, a silly grin,
The sprinkle load, we wear like skin.
We giggle loud, trip on our feet,
And declare our quest for something sweet.

Marshmallow fluff on every nose,
A sticky mess, as laughter grows.
We'll build a fort with gumdrops tall,
A gingerbread house, we'll have a ball.

In dreams of sweets, we drift away,
To whimsical lands where we can play.
With every bite, the world feels right,
As stars above guide our delight.

Ginger-Scented Secrets

Whispers float on cinnamon air,
With secrets shared, we watch and stare.
The cookie jar has tales to tell,
Of midnight snacks and sugar spells.

While nibbling crumbs we spin our yarns,
Of cookie kings and ginger charms.
A royal feast, a sugar dance,
Everything's better when there's a chance.

In candy capes, we save the day,
With licorice ropes, we swing and sway.
Giggles echo where sweets collide,
Our merry tale we cannot hide.

So grab a seat, come take a slice,
Life's best enjoyed when soft and nice.
With frosted dreams, we'll toast tonight,
To sugary wishes, pure delight!

Winter's Sweet Embrace

Snowflakes dance in the glow,
Chocolate chips in tow.
Bundled up, we roam,
In search of cookie-y scrumptious home.

Winter's chill makes us grin,
As flour flies on the din.
Laughter echoes through the air,
While frosting ends up in our hair.

Mittens lost, what a sight,
Slippery tiles, oh what a fright!
With each bite comes delight,
Sledding with cookies feels so right.

So gather round, come share a bite,
On this winter evening bright.
With each giggle and each crumb,
Our fun-filled night's begun!

Cookies and Candlelight

Scent of sugar fills the air,
Rolling dough without a care.
With sprinkles falling like rain,
We laugh and dance with sweet refrain.

Candle flickers, shadows play,
We'll bake our worries away.
Iced the reindeer, oh what fun,
They're not just for Christmas, oh no, none!

Flour on our cheeks, so bold,
Our cookie tales are worth their gold.
With each batch comes a jest,
Who knew baking could be a quest?

So here's to winter, frosty and bright,
With cookies and friends, it feels just right.
Let's sing and munch till the morning light,
In this cozy, warm delight.

Whispers of Spiced Delight

Ginger snaps and nutmeg cheer,
Chasing friends all around here.
With every laugh, a spice we blend,
In this mirth, we shall not end.

Merry tales on the snowy lane,
We prank each other, they're our gain.
Cookies fly through the night sky,
'Till we all collapse, laughing like pie.

Muffins hiding, missing a few,
They've run off with the blueberry stew!
A dash of fun in every bite,
As we munch till the morning light.

So sing with me this spiced affair,
Let's make a mess without a care.
With sugar plums tucked in dreams,
We'll feast till morning, or so it seems.

The Sugarplum Moon

Up above, a moon so sweet,
Decorated with fruity treats.
We dance beneath its glowing beams,
Collecting laughter, or so it seems.

Sprinkles falling from the skies,
While cookies wave, oh how they sigh.
With every crunch, we giggle loud,
In this festive, joyous crowd.

Nights of mischief spun with glee,
Marshmallow snowball fights, you see.
As frosting trails on our faces bright,
Each bite brings whispers of delight.

So raise your glasses, toast tonight,
To sugary dreams taking flight.
In the warmth of friends and cheer,
We'll chase the fun, year after year!

The Stars' Sugary Embrace

Under the twinkling skies, they dance,
With sugar rushes, they take a chance.
A comet slips on icing slick,
While clumsy elves perform a trick.

Jingle bells mix with laughter loud,
As ginger folks gather, oh so proud.
Marshmallow hats fly through the air,
Landing softly without a care.

Sugar plums giggle, feeling spry,
While peppermint fairies zoom on by.
They trip over gumdrops, full of cheer,
Adding sweetness to the cold night here.

A cupcake cloud drifts in the night,
With frosting smiles that feel just right.
The starry sprinkle dust takes flight,
In this zany, sugary delight.

A Quilt of Cookie Warmth

Baking dreams on a snowy eve,
With cookie crumbs, we easily cleave.
A blanket of chocolate chip bites,
Wraps us up on these cozy nights.

Rolling dough, oh what a sight,
Giggling cooks with flour fight.
A sprinkle battle breaks the peace,
Flour everywhere, laughter won't cease.

Marzipan creatures do a dance,
Dodging sprinkles, they take their chance.
A cookie cat jumps and trips,
Sending frosting from his hips.

In this warm, sugary embrace,
Crumbles of joy, we shall not waste.
A quilt so sweet, with laughter spun,
Each bite, a giggle, oh what fun!

The Winter Whisk of Delight

With every whip, the chaos grows,
In a bowl where laughter flows.
The whisk spins tales of sugary cheer,
Bringing giggles of joy, oh dear!

Batter splatters like winter snow,
While grandma laughs, "Oh no, oh no!"
A touch of cinnamon fills the air,
As we mix up madness without a care.

Time to bake the tales we share,
With doughy creatures everywhere.
A cookie monkey swings in fright,
Declaring it a cookie fight!

Oh taste the fun, oh feel the zest,
As winter's whisk puts us to the test.
In this kitchen filled with delight,
We bake more giggles every night.

Celestial Cinnamon Hues

Stars made of sugar, bright and fair,
Turn cinnamon swirls into the air.
A cosmic dance with cake and spice,
In this galaxy, everything's nice.

Laughter erupts from chocolate moons,
While cookie comets sing sweet tunes.
A brownie black hole, oh what a plight,
Sucking in treats, a delicious bite!

The sugar rush builds with every swing,
As marshmallows explode, what joy they bring!
A confetti star shower glows,
Filling our hearts as the sweetness grows.

In the cosmos of laughter, we cheer,
With each sugary twinkle drawing near.
Cinnamon scents fill the frosty blue,
In this heavenly night, just me and you.

The Twilight Icing

Under the glow of kitchen lights,
Cookies chat and play silly fights.
Rolling pins dance, flour in the air,
Laughter bubbles, no time for a care.

Spices whisper secrets so grand,
While candy canes protect their land.
The whisk makes jokes, a comedic tool,
In the sweet chaos, we laugh like fools.

A Glimpse into a Sugar Soul

Cinnamon dreams swirl round the bowl,
Marshmallows bounce, each with a goal.
Gumdrop giggles, in rainbow hues,
Sharing tales of sugar-sweet views.

Fudge blocks trade their comical puns,
While licorice laces have frolicsome runs.
In this sugary world, joy takes its toll,
As we peek inside a candy-filled soul.

Magic Lurks in Bakery Shadows

In the quiet of night, a doughnut sighs,
Puffed-up pastry dreams of skies.
The oven hums a whimsical tune,
As cupcakes plot under the glowing moon.

Brownies giggle, spreading delight,
With frosting hats, they dance through the night.
Behind the counters, delights come alive,
In shadowy corners, sweet laughter will thrive.

The Spirit of Cozy Confection

A marshmallow snowy on cocoa's throne,
Laughing with cookies, not feeling alone.
Ginger snaps tease, in a never-ending race,
While pies wink with a flaky embrace.

Whipped cream clouds float in the night,
Chanting songs with sweet and light.
In the cozy warmth, we gather around,
As sugary spirits in laughter abound.

Sweet Hues of Winter's Kiss

In a kitchen filled with cheer,
Sugar sprinkles disappear.
Rolling, cutting, giggles galore,
Flour fights, oh, what a chore!

With icing swirls of bright delight,
Cookies winking, oh what a sight!
Candies tumble, laughter flows,
Who knew baking comes with shows?

The whisk is wielded like a sword,
While ginger snickers at the hoard.
All the flavors mix and sway,
In this winter's merry play!

As crumbs fly out, we make a mess,
Yet taste each batch, no time to guess.
Every bite's a frosty jest,
Winter's kiss is simply the best!

The Night the Cookies Danced

Under twinkling stars so bright,
Cookies think it's time for flight.
With frosting hats and gumdrop shoes,
They gather round for festive blues.

The peanut butter crew arrives,
Nutty jokes and clumsy jives.
Chocolate chips in the spotlight beam,
Busting moves like in a dream!

Spicing things up with ginger flair,
Brown sugar churns with wild hair.
Twists and twirls in the moonlight glow,
Laughter echoes, stealing the show!

But one rogue tart, with a frosting smile,
Gained the spotlight with candy style.
As night unfolds, so sweetly pranced,
The cookies truly had their chance!

Memories Served on Icy Platters

On a platter cold and bright,
Memories of sheer delight.
With frosted dreams, we reminisce,
Each cookie brings a frosty kiss!

Bite by bite, we twirl and laugh,
Sharing stories on our crafty path.
Sprinkled tales of past delight,
As laughter dances through the night!

Peppermint whispers of the fun,
Marshmallow fluff battles, one by one.
We serve it up with love and cheer,
Each bite a burst of yesteryear!

The chilly air wraps us so tight,
In sugary warmth, we unite.
With each taste, our hearts combine,
On icy platters, memories shine!

Candlelit Moments in a Sugar Wonderland

In a wonderland of sweet delight,
Candles flicker, oh what a sight!
Frosted hills and sugar trees,
Whiskers twitch with the winter breeze.

Every corner holds a treat,
Sticky fingers can't be beat!
Sipping cocoa by the glow,
This is where the laughter flows.

Marzipan moons hang low and round,
Bonbon echoes are the sound.
Candied laughter fills the air,
Sugar dreams bring tales to share!

As we gather 'round the warmth,
With sugary snacks, we find our charm.
In this whimsical, sweet embrace,
Moments linger, time to chase!

Kisses of Nutmeg and Ice

Sugar plums dance, a twinkle in the air,
Sprinkled laughter, shimmering everywhere.
Frosty faces, cheeks red and round,
Wobbling like jelly, joyfully unbound.

Cookies jingle as they take a stroll,
With candy cane canes, a silly soul.
Gingerbread men, they're plotting a prank,
Chasing each other around the dashed plank.

Witty whispers from the marshmallow crowd,
Making snow angels, giggling so loud.
A dance with sprinkles, oh what a sight,
In the silly snow under the soft moonlight.

The Sweet Poetry of Winter Walls

Walls adorned with syrupy twine,
Whipped cream dreams on a sugar line.
Laughter echoes like a chiming bell,
While chocolate crumbs tell their own tale.

Frosty windows, a masterpiece grins,
Mischief hiding behind layers of sins.
Candy hearts whisper secrets of cheer,
As each snowy flake drifts in and near.

Scent of vanilla, it tickles the nose,
While gumdrops giggle as winter wind blows.
Icing drizzled on stories we weave,
In sweet winter wonder, we joyfully grieve.

Iced Epiphanies Underneath the Stars

Under twinkling shimmer, ideas collide,
Clouds of cinnamon swirling with pride.
Bright sparks of laughter, sprinkle the night,
As chipmunk DJs prepare for a fright!

Cold cheeks glowing, with gingerbread cheer,
As frosts cackle softly, drawing us near.
Snowmen gossip under starlit skies,
While playful snowflakes dance in disguise.

Epiphany stirs in a cup of hot drink,
Where marshmallows plop, and we never think.
The stars conspire with minty delight,
Crafting sweet chaos on this frosty night.

Sugar-Dusted Journeys

On a sleigh ride through the sweet, snowy haze,
   Where giggles and sugar are all the craze.
   Chasing the laughter, we tumble and roll,
In this sugary wonder, we lose all control.

Winding paths covered in glittery dust,
   In biscuit towns with candy we trust.
Marzipan meadows and licorice streams,
We savor the chaos that warms up our dreams.

Sipping from cupfuls of joy and of glee,
With frosting on noses, how silly we be!
   Each frosty journey a story to hold,
   As treasures unfold, all glittering gold.

The Warmth of Cinnamon Glow

In the kitchen, sweet chaos reigns,
Flour flies like snow, oh what a mess!
The cat leaps high, a flying fluff ball,
While I battle dough, feeling like less.

Rolling pins dance, what a wild sight,
Sugar sprinkles, they shimmer and spin.
A runaway cookie darts to the left,
With laughter bubbling up from within.

The oven hums a cheerful tune,
While I play hopscotch with pie plates galore.
With each sweet bite, goofy grins spread,
Who knew baking could be such a chore?

So grab a whisk, let's join the fun,
Mixing giggles in every swirl.
In this warm chaos, joy is the goal,
Baked with love, it's a jolly whirl!

Starry Cookies on the Hearth

Under twinkling lights, we gather 'round,
A plate of stars, not quite round!
With sprinkles that dance like they're in a show,
These cookies are stars, now watch 'em glow.

We sprinkle the flour, and then it goes,
Right down my shirt, right on my nose!
Friends start to giggle, I'm a floury sight,
With cheeky grins, we mix 'til it's right.

Rolling out dough like it's a grand song,
Each cutout's a tune that we sing along.
Some shapes end up looking rather bizarre,
Tastes so funny, they're cookies by far!

So gather your crew, let merriment flow,
As we bake up some joy, let the laughter grow.
With each starry treat that we munch and we bite,
This baking party is pure delight!

Chilled Sweets and Cozy Beats

Chilled sweets abound in this frosty delight,
As we whip up fun on a chilly night.
With melodies in air, we mix and we muse,
Making treats that sparkle like shiny shoes.

The chocolate chips, oh, they tease and they taunt,
Leading my taste buds on a cookie hunt.
Each one a giggle, a sweet little song,
In this cozy kitchen, we feel we belong.

With spoons as our instruments, we stir and we blend,
Every bite, a punchline that makes laughter ascend.
A dash of mishaps, a sprinkle of play,
In this doughy symphony, joy leads the way!

So roll out the laughter, let happiness flow,
With chilled sweets and fun, let the good times grow.
For each silly creation brings smiles out loud,
In a conference of cookies, we're all so proud!

Nibbles of Nostalgia

As we nibble on memories baked from the past,
The scents swirl around, these moments won't last.
With crumbly edges and sweet, gooey hearts,
Each bite tells a story, where laughter imparts.

Oh, the times we spent with flour in hair,
Mixing up stories with love in the air.
Chocolate smudges mark the days gone by,
Like happy little flags, they lift up the sky.

In the giggles and snorts, we find our delight,
With each frosted mishap, we cherish the night.
So let's raise a spoon to this flavorful fight,
Celebrating together, our hearts feel so light!

With nibbles of joy and sprinkles of cheer,
We bake up the memories, each moment so dear.
In this cozy kitchen, where time flies and spins,
We gather for laughter, where sweet life begins!

Frosty Ember Serenade

In the kitchen, chaos reigns,
A cookie monster's joy remains.
Sprinkles fly like tiny stars,
As flour travels, oh how far!

Rolling dough with giggles sweet,
The taste test makes it quite a treat.
The oven hums a cheerful tune,
While doughy bits dance with the moon.

Silly shapes, a lopsided grin,
A gingerbread man wearing a pin.
We laugh as we lose the frosting fight,
With candy canes that seem too bright.

The kitchen's a whirlwind, a giggle spree,
Who knew baking could be so zany?
With frosted smiles and merry hearts,
The fun of making is where it starts!

The Enchantment of Iced Delights

Sugar clouds float in the air,
Giggling elves, without a care.
A half-baked dream, they're up to pranks,
With toothy grins and wobbly flanks.

Whiskers dipped in chocolate glaze,
Bewitched by the tasty ways.
Ginger snaps that dance on plates,
A sight that really celebrates.

Muffin caps and cookie hats,
Dancing with our furry cats.
Each treat holds a secret dare,
To take a nibble, if you dare!

Sprinkled laughter fills our space,
With frosting plopped on every face.
In this realm of sweet delight,
Even the veggies seem polite!

Starry Confections Under Moonlight

Doughnuts dangle like the stars,
In a galaxy of sugary jars.
A marshmallow moon looks quite surprised,
At the cookie party, full of pies!

Sugar cloves make quite the mess,
As we laugh and can't guess,
Which treats will wobble as we take a bite,
Creating giggles in the shimmering night.

Sprinkled stars in every hue,
Candy canes for me and you.
With every crunch and fluffy cheer,
The laughter swirls, bringing cheer.

Cupcakes twerk and brownies sing,
As cupcake wars are the real thing.
In a world of treats where munchies reign,
Who knew sugar could drive us insane?

Cinnamon Wishes on Silent Streets

Snowflakes fall with a gentle sound,
While spice-laden dreams dance around.
Muffins tumble off the shelf,
As we chuckle, like a happy elf.

Whipped cream plops in a soft delight,
On reindeer cookies, a comical sight.
Nibbled treats from every home,
Frosted giggles when we roam.

Sugar sprinkles in the air,
As snowmen wink without a care.
With every bite a joke unfolds,
A laughter cozy, bright, and bold.

The streets alive with yummy cheer,
As we scamper, tummies near.
Cinnamon wishes sprinkled bright,
In this season, joy takes flight!

Yuletide Whimsy Unwrapped

In a kitchen filled with cheer,
A cookie monster draws near.
With a whisk and a twirl,
He makes flour fly and twirl.

Sugar sprinkles rain like snow,
And the laughter starts to flow.
Baking blunders make us gleeful,
Though the dough be slightly lethal.

A candy cane fight draws near,
While the cat jumps in with cheer.
All the frosting is a mess,
But it's fun—no need to stress!

So gather 'round, let's not delay,
For holiday silliness, hooray!
With giggles loud and hearts so bright,
We'll feast on treats this joyous night.

Glimmering Frost on Sugar Crusts

Cookies glisten on the rack,
But as they cool, they plan attack.
The ginger men lift up their heads,
While visions dance in cookie beds.

A rogue sprig of mistletoe,
Hangs low; now chaos starts to flow.
Frosting fights and chuckles loud,
Turn the night into a crowd.

Someone's slipping on a plume,
Of flour dust—a snowy room!
Laughter echoes, sugar highs,
As dough balls take to the skies!

Chasing laughter, rolling rounds,
With giggling joy that still astounds.
In the kitchen, hearts in flight,
We'll bake more mischief tonight!

Moonlit Recipes for the Soul

Under the stars, we mix and blend,
With sprinkles that never seem to end.
A dash of humor, a splash of fun,
In a pot of laughter, we have just begun.

Whiskers twitch as the flour flies,
Elves of chaos in disguise.
The clock ticks loud, it shouts with glee,
"Bake more cookies; come play with me!"

Snowflakes join the silly dance,
While sweet dough takes a chance.
Rolling pins and sugar fights,
Make the best of winter nights!

So gather 'round, bring your cheer,
With warm cookies and friends so dear.
In this moonlit kitchen glow,
We're masters of the baking show!

Spice-Infused Echoes of December

Cinnamon whispers in the air,
As we dance around without a care.
Laughter fills the cozy room,
While cookie storms begin to bloom.

An army of flour, a battleground,
With spritz cookies making silly sounds.
A showdown of sweet, the stakes are high,
As gingerbread men start to fly!

A milk moustache, a frosting fight,
With giggles echoing through the night.
Swirling flavors, sweet and bold,
In December's chill, we break the mold.

So take a bite, enjoy the cheer,
Another batch; let's bake some here!
With spice-infused secrets, we delight,
Creating treasures through the night!

Frosted Twilight Confections

In a kitchen, chaos reigns with cheer,
Flour on noses, laughter fills the sphere.
Cookie shapes dance, no two are the same,
One looks like a dog, and one—what a shame!

Spices jump and twirl, a sweet ballet,
Ginger leaps high, the nutmeg wants to play.
The dough goes rolling, oh what a sight!
The oven's a monster, ready to bite!

Little sprinkles rain, like colorful skies,
Frosting mustache on a baker's prize.
The timer dings loudly, the cookies cheer,
"Who ate that last one?" it's still unclear!

With giggles and crumbs, our work here is done,
The taste-test brigade finds it all too fun.
Sugar high and silly grins glow bright,
Another round of chaos, oh what a night!

A Recipe for Starry Nights

Gather 'round, friends, for a tasty delight,
With flour and sugar, we'll create our night.
Mix in some giggles, a dash of good cheer,
Stir with a wink, and watch your cares disappear.

Ginger, oh ginger, you sneaky old spice,
What secrets you bring, how could you be nice?
Baking's not rocket science, they all said,
But flour explosions left all filled with dread!

The dough takes a rest, with giggly delight,
While shapes form like stars, a whimsical sight.
Chocolate chip comets and sprinkles that sing,
Commands of the kitchen give sweet joy to bring.

As our cookies arise, like dreams in the sky,
The oven's hot breath makes our spirits fly.
'Til midnight we'll taste, with smiles shining bright,
Who knew that cooking could bring such pure light?

The Gathering of Winter's Treats

A party of flavors, they all come alive,
Nutty and sugary, they buzz and they jive.
The candy canes shimmy, the gumdrops take flight,
The peanut brittle snaps, oh what a wild night!

Marshmallows are bouncing, they're caught in the mix,
With licorice lingo and sugar-filled tricks.
We whip up a storm; the kitchen's a scene,
Cinnamon twirls with a marzipan gleam.

Baking is bonding; it's sweet laughter's art,
Each bite holds a memory; it's all from the heart.
The frosting's the laughter; the sprinkles, our glee,
This winter's collection makes joyous all we see.

With snacks piled high, like mountains of fun,
We munch and we chat, until night's almost done.
Each morsel a treasure, each smile a treat,
A gathering of joy, oh, what more could we eat?

A Meeting of Spice and Chill

In the heart of winter, the spices convene,
Chillies are crackling, a riotous scene.
Gingerbread gossip, oh what will they share?
The nutmeg recounts how it danced in the air.

Frosting's on standby, it's ready to play,
Mingling with sugars in a frothy ballet.
The marshmallows giggle, don't take it too hard,
As they plan a heist of the sugar-filled yard!

Cookies clash with sprinkles, in a sweet little fray,
Tears made of laughter that warm the cold day.
A sprinkle-top hat on a wobbly cake,
It's madness and magic for dessert's sake!

So gather the spices, let the spice wars cease,
For every sweet moment brings us closer, at least.
Laughter and treats, oh, what a grand thrill,
In this funny little world of chill and of spice!

Sugar Dust on the Frozen Path

Slipping and sliding with each merry step,
Giggling softly as we start to prep.
Snowflakes sprinkle like sugar on cake,
Watch out for the snowman we're bound to make!

With carrots for noses and eyes made of coal,
His smile is crooked but plays a great role.
As we toss snowballs, a flurry in flight,
A giggling battle, oh what a delight!

Dreams Wrapped in Brown Sugar

Under the moon with its chilly breath,
We whisper secrets, not minding the theft.
Cookies are waiting, stacked high on a plate,
But oh, that one crumb, it's attracting our fate!

The dog comes a-tumbling, a shadowy blur,
In a moment of chaos, oh how we concur!
With icing on noses and laughter so bright,
Our dreams dance around in the ephemeral night!

The Spirit of Frosty Evenings

We gather 'round hijinks, each friend with a grin,
As we share our tales of holiday sin.
Laughter erupts as we sip on hot cocoa,
Straws made of candy, oh what a good show!

A marshmallow snowman, he's plopping about,
Each wobble and wobble ends with a shout.
With winter's chill biting, we keep spirits high,
On this frosty evening, we'll laugh till we cry!

Holiday Frosting and Fable

In the kitchen, the chaos begins to form,
With sprinkles and laughter, it's all quite the norm.
An explosion of color on cookies galore,
Each bite brings a chuckle, can't ask for more!

The pet cat looks suspicious, eyeing the fun,
Will she have frosting, or just take a run?
Our tales twist like icing, with giggles and mess,
In this sugary fable, we surely are blessed!

A Glimpse of Spiced Harmony

In the kitchen, scents collide,
Dough men dancing, with arms wide.
Ovens blazing, timers beep,
Laughter echoes, none lose sleep.

Rolling pins take flight and twirl,
Flour fights in an epic swirl.
Cookies giggle on the tray,
Who knew sweets would have their say?

Frosting spears and gumdrop fights,
Sugar highs reach dizzying heights.
Chuckle-fests of sweet delight,
Innocent joy ignites the night.

Now the world falls sweetly still,
Dreams of icing, hearts to thrill.
Spiced harmony in every bite,
A symphony, which feels just right.

The Magic of Sweet Confections

Candy canes and peppermint,
Mischief wrapped in a sweet scent.
Chocolate rivers flow so deep,
Gummy bears jump, never sleep.

Whiskers twitch from crafty cats,
Dancing crumbs attract the rats.
Syrup spills and stories rise,
Silly tales wrapped in surprise.

Cupcake castles, frosting kings,
Nonsense wraps in sugary bling.
With every laugh, the sweets conspire,
A world aflame with tasty fire.

Laughter dances on the air,
Sweet confections everywhere.
Magic's found in every crumb,
Join the feast, let laughter hum!

Starlit Recipes of Delight

Under a sky with sparkling cheer,
Culinary dreams draw ever near.
A sprinkle here, a dash of that,
Doughy mischief, where's the cat?

Whisking away the stiffest cream,
In a bowl, we dare to dream.
Riotous flavors blend and gleam,
Starlit joy, a glorious theme.

Chocolate chips and fruity bites,
A culinary haze ignites.
Tickling noses draws delight,
Silly dances in the night.

Recipes woven with giggles tight,
Sweet enchantments take their flight.
In every bite, a laugh is found,
Unraveled joy, all around.

A Symphony of Sweetness

Gather round, the table's set,
A symphony we won't regret.
Jam-filled crescendos rise and fall,
Gingerbread men, they stand tall.

Bubbles pop from fizzy drinks,
Lemon zings and peppermint blinks.
Spoons are dancing, forks collide,
A taste explosion, come inside!

Frothy laughs in every sip,
Taste the triumph on each trip.
Chocolate drizzles, colors bright,
Sweets compose a pure delight.

So raise a glass to irony,
In every bite, a mystery.
A symphony of sweets tonight,
Join the feast, it feels so right!

The Warmth of Homemade Comfort

In the kitchen, a ruckus soon forms,
Flour dances like snow in the storms.
With doughy hands, we craft and we mold,
Mom's secret recipe, a treasure of old.

Laughter echoes as we sneak a bite,
Chocolate chips gleam in the soft, warm light.
A whisk goes flying, oh what a scene,
Sugar and spice, in chaos we gleam.

The oven hums like a cheerful friend,
Patiently waiting for moments to blend.
My sister squeals as the timer dings,
Out come the treats, oh what joy it brings!

Cinnamon giggles tickle the air,
As we gather 'round without a care.
With every munch, our worries take flight,
In the warmth of comfort, all feels just right.

Tinsel and Vanilla Dreams

A sprinkle of tinsel, a dash of delight,
Vanilla wafts softly in the glimmering night.
Cookies adorned with sequins of cheer,
Each one a wonder, each one a dear.

The dog steals a treat, oh, what a sight,
We all stop and giggle, it's pure delight.
Almost like magic, the mess that we make,
Flour on the floor, a hilarious quake!

Our laughter pops like the fizz of a drink,
As we orchestrate flavors, and winks with a wink.
A jolly old snowman joins in the fun,
His belly's so round, you might think he'd run!

In the chaos of butter and sprinkles that gleam,
We feast like there's no tomorrow, it seems.
With hearts filled with joy and tinsel galore,
Each cookie's a story, who could ask for more?

Frostbitten Lullabies of Joy

Under the moonlight, sweet laughter takes flight,
Cookies are missing, oh what a sight!
A giggle escapes as we hunt through the space,
The pets are suspicious; there's crumbs on their face.

Snowflakes are falling, the backyard's ablaze,
With laughter of children lost in a maze.
We build up a snowman, but he's quite a flop,
His carrot nose wobbles, then takes a big drop!

We cozy up close with cocoa in hand,
As marshmallows float, oh isn't it grand?
The snowman agrees with a nod of his head,
He joins us in laughter, as he's not quite dead!

With stories that twinkle like stars up above,
The warmth that we share, oh how we do love.
Each giggling moment, a treasure, oh yes,
In this frosty embrace, we feel truly blessed.

The Last Cookie on the Plate

One lone cookie remains on the tray,
It's tempting and crispy, in a mischievous way.
We ponder its fate, should we take the risk?
Or will it vanish in a chocolatey mist?

My brother's approaching with a sly little grin,
He lifts up the plate, oh where to begin?
A game of decision, we stare and we play,
The cookie grows colder, it's wasting away!

With a wink and a nudge, we dive right in,
A battle of giggles, oh, let the fun begin!
The last chunk of sweetness, we tumble and fight,
In the name of dessert, oh what a delight!

Crumbs flying wildly, we savor the bite,
Just two silly kids in the warm, cozy night.
With laughter and crumbs on our faces so bright,
We treasure this cookie, our ultimate rite.

Twilight Treats and Tinsel Tales

Under twinkling lights we snack,
With cookies shaped like a cheerful quack.
Giggles burst like jingle bells,
As icing tales and sweet smells swell.

A frosting fight? Oh, what a scene!
Our faces all dressed in sugary sheen.
The laughter echoes, a jolly din,
In our little world, where we all win.

Sprinkled spritzers and ginger snaps,
Caught in antics, no time for naps!
Elves in the corner roll their eyes,
At our delightful, messy surprise.

So raise your mugs of hot cocoa cheer,
Toast to the season, to fun and good beer!
For under these stars, we're silly and bright,
In twilight treats and tinsel delight.

The Enchantment of Icing Canvas

A canvas laid with icing spread,
We paint our cookies rather than bed.
With candy canes we draw a scene,
Of dancing bears, oh what a dream!

Baking artsy masterpieces,
With spry little hands, the fun increases.
A sprinkle here, a swirl, a laugh,
Our ginger-genius turns out daft.

The kitten strolls across our joys,
In a zig-zag, oh, what a ploy!
With a swipe of paw, artistic fate,
Our gallery's now a cat-tastrophe state!

But in this chaos, sweet smiles grow,
Our favorite moments, a splendid show.
So gather 'round, let's taste our art,
In this enchanting tale where silliness starts.

Seasonal Smiles and Warm Scents

In the kitchen, warmth surrounds,
With laughter bursting, joy abounds.
The oven hums a happy tune,
While scents of cinnamon fill the room.

We mix and blend with floury glee,
Dancing around like tipsy bees.
"Oops, a spill!" we all exclaim,
As sugar storms replace our fame.

The clock strikes hours, yet we're awry,
Our cookie kingdom's pushing the sky.
With cheerful bites and sprinkles rare,
Each cookie whispers, "We don't care!"

So dive into this festive fun,
With all our giggles, we will run.
For seasonal smiles that never fade,
In every laugh, sweet memories made.

Impressions of Sugar Frost on Cold Glass

Through frosted panes we peep outside,
Where snowflakes dance, full of pride.
A world so white, all bright and spry,
With marshmallow fluff clouds drifting by.

Inside our fortress, we sip and grin,
With cookies stacked, we dive right in.
The gingerbread men don't stand a chance,
When we bring out the frosting for a trance!

A mistletoe mishap leads to squeals,
Laughter echoes, joy that heals.
Frosty windows can't hide our play,
In sugary fun, we spend the day.

So here's to chaos, warmth, and cheer,
To moments cherished when friends are near.
Impressions made 'neath twinkling stars,
In sugar-coated fun, who needs a car?

A Blanket of Spice in Midnight's Glow

In the kitchen, flour flies,
A whisk in hand, with joyful cries.
Baking treats, the oven's hum,
Smells so sweet, oh here they come!

Mice join in the midnight feast,
Cuddling close, they're quite the beast.
Rolling pins and laughter blend,
Frosted snacks, the perfect trend.

Sprinkles dance, a playful sight,
Ginger folks in pure delight.
Pies and cookies, what a show,
In the warm, inviting glow.

Laughter bubbles, cocoa spills,
With each bite, we're feeling thrills.
A blanket of spice upon our lap,
Happiness wrapped in a sugary trap.

The Joy of Baked Wonders Unfolds.

Rolling dough, with a touch of sass,
Flour puff clouds as we pass.
Mixing nuts, and cinnamon too,
Oh, what wonders we will brew!

In the corner, a curious cat,
Eyeing cookies, imagine that!
With a twitch of her furry tail,
Plans of mischief start to sail.

A sprinkle here, a drizzle there,
Icing battles fill the air.
With each flavor, giggles rise,
Sugar highs bring brightened eyes.

The timer dings, oh what a sound,
Baked delights, we gather 'round.
Laughter echoes, warmth unfolds,
This sweet life is worth its gold.

Whispers of Winter's Spice

In a corner, cozy and small,
Baking spices make their call.
Nutmeg whispers, cloves do dance,
In this kitchen, we take a chance.

Mixing butter, sugar, glee,
The smell of joy, come smell with me!
Frosty windows, giggles flow,
What's in the pot? Let's wait and know.

Friends gather round, in warm embrace,
Chewing on treats, no time to waste.
Fluffy marshmallows join the cheer,
Hot cocoa flows, let's bring it here!

In this season, laughter roams,
As we create our perfect homes.
Whispers of spice fill up the night,
With every bite, our hearts take flight.

Sugar-Coated Dreams

Baking dreams in a sugar coat,
Frosting waves upon our boat.
Piping laughter through the air,
Every cookie made with care.

Sprinkled tales of whipped delight,
Merry chaos, a tasty fight.
Here comes chocolate, right on cue,
Glazed with giggles, just for you.

Tiny hands, with doughy mess,
Somehow ends in a sweet success.
Faces covered, floury grin,
In this game, there's never a sin!

Sugar-coated dreams abound,
Joy is found in every round.
With a wink and frosted cheer,
Let's bake more joy throughout the year!

The Dance of Crystallized Joy

In a land where sweets collide,
The gumball kings all joyfully bide.
Marshmallow clouds float on by,
As candied rainbows fill the sky.

Sprinkles fall like winter's laugh,
While jellies dance on candy-craft.
The chocolate river flows so bright,
As gumdrops twirl with sheer delight.

Lollipops take on a ballet sway,
Sugar fairies leap and play.
Frosty giggles bubble in the air,
With every spin, there's something rare.

When the clock strikes a sugary tone,
Sugarplum dreams are brightly sewn.
Join the fun, let laughter grow,
In this land where sweet things flow.

A Sugarplum Pathway

Down a candy lane so sweet,
Where jellybeans and chocolate meet.
Ginger marionettes prance around,
As laughter bubbles from the ground.

Cotton candy clouds are near,
With licorice trees that stand so clear.
Bubblegum shoes help you glide,
On this pathway of joy and pride.

Soda pop fountains sprinkle cheer,
With every sip, all worries disappear.
Lollipop signs point the way,
To playful dreams that love to sway.

Join the march of candy sprites,
Beneath a glow of carousel lights.
Each step is filled with silly charms,
On this pathway that sweetly warms.

When Nightingale Sang of Sugar

A nightingale took flight so high,
Singing songs that made folks cry.
Of lollipops and licorice dreams,
Making hearts burst at the seams.

With every chirp, a candy treat,
Gumdrops scattered at our feet.
Marzipan moons hung in the sky,
As giggles echoed, oh so sly.

Peanut brittle danced across the stage,
In this sweet, whimsical page.
A dreamland made of sugar and fun,
When nightingale's song had just begun.

Join the choirs of fluffy clouds,
Where laughter sparkles and joy enshrouds.
Every note a sweet delight,
As we celebrate this joyous night.

Hearts Wrapped in Marzipan

In a village bright with gleeful cheer,
Candy hearts whisper, 'Come near.'
Wrapped in marzipan's gentle hold,
Their stories of sweetness are lovingly told.

Banana peels slip with glee,
As gumdrops giggle in harmony.
The peppermint breeze brings a smile,
And candy canes dance every while.

With a wink and a sprinkle of sweet,
Every heart skips a jubilant beat.
In this land where laughter beams,
Life is filled with candy dreams.

So gather 'round, don't be shy,
As we soar under the cream-puff sky.
Hearts wrapped in treats boldly sing,
Celebrating joy that candies bring.

Scented Whirls of Joy

Whisking flour like a dance,
I tripped and left a messy chance.
Sugar piled up, what a sight,
Sweet disaster, oh what a plight!

Sprinkles flew like confetti bright,
Cookies giggled in pure delight.
I asked the dough to make a friend,
It just rolled away; the dough did bend!

Baking tales of laughter swell,
In this kitchen, all is well.
Laughter tastes like chocolate chips,
While the oven hums and quips!

Scented dreams swirl through the air,
I'll wear cookies like warm underwear.
With every bite, I giggle and grin,
In a world where the frosting won't thin!

The Flavor of Midnight Snowfall

In the moonlight, cookies shine,
Frosting rivers, oh what a line!
Gingerbread men in a silly race,
Falling flat with a whipped cream face!

Snowflakes sprinkle on my plate,
I'm too late; they just can't wait!
Minty marshmallows do the twist,
Dancing on hot cocoa, can't resist!

A pinch of salt and a dash of glee,
Sipping chocolate with a honeybee.
Giggles burst like candy canes,
In this flavor realm, nothing wanes!

Winter's magic, a tasty spree,
Each laugh warms my chilly spree.
With every sip, my heart takes flight,
Oh, the joy of sweet delight!

Spirits of the Season's Bake

Flour ghosts in the cooling air,
Sugar spirits sit everywhere.
Rolling pins start to jive,
With every whack, the cookies thrive!

Oh, the chaos that fills my mind,
Flour-dusted friends, find the time!
Sugar cones in a towering heap,
Sleepless nights, but I don't weep!

Chocolates melt, oh sweet release,
While candy hearts join in the feast.
Whisking dreams like frothy waves,
As the oven hums and saves!

Laughter echoes through the town,
Baking's fun when you wear a frown.
Spirits soar; don't have to bake,
Just let joy in your heart awake!

A Cup of Cocoa Under Stars

Stargazing with a mug so round,
Cocoa spills without a sound.
Whipped cream clouds float above my chin,
As silly thoughts dance and spin!

Marshmallow peeps all dressed in white,
Do a jig, what a funny sight!
Skating on the chocolate sea,
Cocoa waves calling to me!

Each sip brings a chuckle free,
Stars wink back, come have a spree!
With candy canes riding in tow,
Here's to giggles and hot cocoa flow!

Under the moon's soft, glowing gaze,
Cup in hand, I'm lost in a daze.
Sipping joy beneath the night,
With every gulp, my heart takes flight!

Twilight Bakehouse Whimsy

In the bakehouse, mice start to groove,
Dancing 'round the cookie dough, trying to move.
Flour clouds swirl, like wintery glee,
As the oven hums sweetly, oh can't you see!

Sprinkles rain down as if from the sky,
Sugar-coated giggles, oh my, oh my!
A rolling pin rolls like it's in a race,
Every pastry a smile, a doughy embrace.

Jolly bakers wear hats far too big,
Twirling and swirling, doing a jig.
While the cupcakes chime sweet little tunes,
Chanting for frosting beneath the moon.

What's that aroma? A prankster's delight!
Mixing up flavors that give quite a fright.
With a pinch of the zany and a dash of the fun,
Twilight bakehouse, it's a party begun!

Crumbs of Celestial Charm

Starlit crumbs scattered on cosmic trails,
Clumsy little critters with gingerbread tails.
Nibbling and giggling beneath the night's shroud,
Squeaky laughter echoes, cheerful and loud.

The moon winks down with a sugary grin,
As moonbeams invite us to spin and spin.
Recipes scribbled in hasty delight,
Divine peanut butter may cause quite a fright.

Saucy concoctions bubble and brew,
Marshmallow moons soaring, oh what a view!
Chocolate chip comets collide in the air,
Twinkling with sweetness beyond compare.

Whiskers of mice with crumbs on their snouts,
Chasing dessert dreams in whimsical bouts.
As sprinkles of laughter fill the sky bright,
The night dances on with delicious delight!

Velvet Chill of Sugary Nights

Gingerbread people in a frolicsome dance,
Wobbling their way in a giggly trance.
Pudding pops twirl with a mischievous hue,
Looking for trouble, those sweets love to brew.

The chilly air swirls with sugar-baked dreams,
Cookies a-chatter, or so it seems.
Candy canes whistle a merry refrain,
Kooky concoctions that tickle the brain.

Lollipop dreams in a wild carousel,
Bakers all smiling, who knew it so well?
Frost-free fun in a whimsical land,
Creativity rumbles, nothing quite as planned.

With a pinch of giggles, a dash of cheer,
Every sweet wonder brings loved ones near.
Under the snowy pastel delight,
Joyous enchantments light up the night!

Sweets Beneath the Starlit Canopy

Beneath a canopy draped with sweet dreams,
Cakes tumble down like colorful streams.
Frosting fights with gravity, how can this be?
Sassy little pastries are wild and free.

Laughter erupts from a licorice lake,
Where gumball trees swirl with each little shake.
Giggles and crumbs float up to the sky,
As jellybeans bounce with a sneeze and a sigh.

Chocolate dread pirates set sail in the night,
Stealing the giggles, oh what a sight!
Whipped cream clouds fluff up the moon's glow,
Twisting and turning in a silly show.

Nutty adventures drift through the air,
Candy-coated whispers with nothing to spare.
Every flavor a riddle, so sweetly sublime,
Join in the fun, it's a sweet-flavored rhyme!

Frosted Lullabies of Joy

Sugar sprinkles fall from the sky,
The cookies wear hats, oh my oh my!
A dancing biscuit twirls with flair,
While marshmallow clouds float through the air.

Chanting ginger snaps, they sing aloud,
The gumdrops giggle, feeling quite proud.
With frosting smiles on every face,
They waltz around in sugary grace.

The milk mustache on a laughing lad,
Brings giggles and cheers—oh, isn't it rad?
With each bite taken, laughter erupts,
As sweet tooth soldiers march and jump.

Beneath the twinkling candy cane lights,
Joy bubbles over on these merry nights.
In a world where sweets reign supreme,
Life is a whimsical, joyful dream.

Whimsy in a Sugar Snowstorm

Sprinkles swirling like a winter gale,
Cookies in scarves tell an epic tale.
The sweets are skidding on the floor,
While chocolate bunnies plan to soar.

With each small hop, there's laughter loud,
As jellybeans join the carefree crowd.
Frosting swirls in the air so bright,
Creating a frosty, silly delight.

Snowmen made of icing, what a sight!
With licorice arms, they dance at night.
Candies chuckle as they roll around,
In this sugary chaos, joy is found.

To the rhythm of a gumdrop beat,
Everyone joins in, tapping their feet.
As sweetness swirls in a laugh-filled spree,
Life is as fun as a candy spree!

Echoes of a Warm Kitchen

Whisking up giggles in a mixing bowl,
Where flour flies and sugar takes hold.
The spatula sings a silly tune,
As cookies dance 'neath the watchful moon.

With each doughy hug, the kids all cheer,
As chocolate chunks draw magic near.
The oven hums a warm, cozy song,
While lively sprinkles cheer all day long.

Tasting the batter, oh what a treat!
The laughter echoes—life is so sweet!
With every batch baked, a smile grows wide,
In this kitchen adventure, joy can't hide.

From cookie sheets to a flour-filled fight,
Silliness reigns in this sweet delight.
As they gather 'round to munch and share,
The kitchen glimmers with laughter everywhere.

Beneath the Icy Canopy

In a world of sugar, where giggles abound,
Under candy trees, joy is found.
Peppermint whispers through the chilled air,
As icicles sparkle—they're quite the fair.

With licorice ropes tying up dreams,
Chocolate chip creeps spill out their schemes.
Nutty delights in a snowy swirl,
As gummy bears twist and twirl.

The chill is a giggle wrapped in delight,
With marshmallow moons shining so bright.
Laughter escapes from a gumdrop cave,
As sweet surprises are what we crave.

In this frosty fun, the joy's all around,
Under sweet canopies, laughter's profound.
As we munch on sprinkles, the night stretches on,
In this witty wonderland, we dance till dawn.

Melodies of Meringue in the Night

In the kitchen, a snicker, a giggle,
The meringue's dancing, with sticky wiggle.
Egg whites are whipping, a fluffy delight,
While spoons play solos in the kitchen light.

Sugar sprinkles rain from above,
As the whisk serenades, oh how it loves!
Flavors colliding, a whimsical fight,
A sugary waltz through the frosty night.

Chocolate chips join in, looking so sly,
Pretending to bake, but they're really just high.
The dough rolls over, it starts to take flight,
With a sprinkle of laughter, oh what a sight!

In this bakery ball, let the world frolic,
Where laughter and sweetness are utterly symbolic.
With each swirling swirl, and each frosty bite,
Melodies linger in the canvas of night.

Symphonies of Sugar and Spice

In the cupboard, a chorus of spice and cheer,
Nutmeg and cinnamon dance without fear.
Flour dusting the floor like fresh winter snow,
A sweet orchestra plays with dough on the go.

Powdered sugar falls like wintery rain,
As laughter erupts through the sugar cane.
Whiskers and giggles fill the air bright,
Creating sweet symphonies deep into night.

The cookie jar jingles with laughter so bold,
As stolen treats turn the kitchen to gold.
Gumdrops are harmonizing, singing their tune,
While cupcakes conspire, under a crescent moon.

From lollipops singing to cakes on the rise,
The pantry plays host to a flurry of pies.
In a sugar-packed dream that feels oh so nice,
We dance in a whirlwind of sugar and spice.

A Frosty Fairytale of Sweetness

In a land where the cookies are ever so bold,
And muffins wear crowns of shimmering gold.
The gingerbread folks prance in the light,
Telling tales of their journeys by the moonlight.

Cupcake cavaliers ride on marshmallow steeds,
While candy canes twirl and chuckle with ease.
The pie takes a bow, with its crust so bright,
In this frosty fairytale, all is just right.

Lollipops croon with a sugary sway,
As frosting-covered castles come out to play.
The syrupy rivers flow bubbly and sweet,
While everyone giggles at gumdrop defeats!

So come take a peek at this whimsical land,
Where sweets hold hands and will always stand.
In this frosting-kissed storybook delight,
Every moment feels like the best of the night.

Lullabies from a Sugarbaker's Dream

In the twilight, the sugarbaker hums,
To the rhythm of frosting and sweet little drums.
Baking up dreams with a sprinkle of laugh,
While the egg timers tap out a silly half.

Chocolate rivers flow through marshmallow hugs,
As gummy bears dance and owner shrugs.
The batter is wiggling, it's dancing with glee,
Under stars that glisten like sweet jubilee.

Whiskers of flour float softly around,
Candy hearts flutter like butterflies found.
The oven sings lullabies, crackling light,
As the cupcakes are dreaming of sugary flight.

So close your eyes tight, let the magic unroll,
In this sweet, frolicking, whimsical stroll.
In a sugarbaker's dream, all is just right,
Where laughter and sweetness embrace through the night.